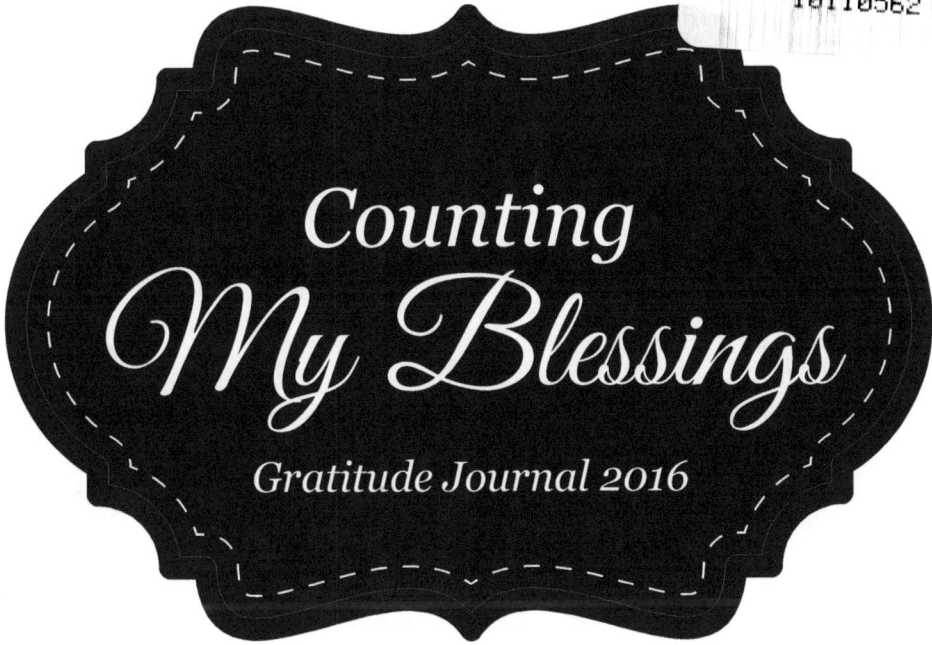

Counting
My Blessings
Gratitude Journal 2016

ACTIVINOTES

Activinotes

DAILY JOURNALS, PLANNERS, NOTEBOOKS AND OTHER BLANK BOOKS

This Book Belongs To

_____

Month of _____

Monthly Focus

Reminders

_____
_____
_____
_____
_____
_____
_____
_____
_____
_____

top three things

1. _____
2. _____
3. _____
4.

_____
_____
_____
_____
_____
_____
_____
_____

Special Dates

_____
_____
_____
_____
_____
_____
_____

_____
_____
_____
_____
_____
_____
_____
_____

home keeping tasks

1. _____
2. _____
3. _____
4. _____

_____
_____
_____
_____
_____
_____

Goals

GOALS FOR THE MONTH

_____

_____ ☐
_____ ☐
_____ ☐
_____ ☐
_____ ☐
_____ ☐

_____

_____ ☐
_____ ☐
_____ ☐
_____ ☐
_____ ☐
_____ ☐

_____

_____ ☐
_____ ☐
_____ ☐
_____ ☐
_____ ☐
_____ ☐
_____ ☐

Daily Gratitude

Date:_____
_____
_____
_____
_____
_____

Date:_____
_____
_____
_____
_____
_____

Date:_____
_____
_____
_____
_____
_____

Date:_____
_____
_____
_____
_____
_____

Date:_____
_____
_____
_____
_____
_____

Date:_____
_____
_____
_____
_____
_____

Date:_____
_____
_____
_____
_____
_____

Date:_____
_____
_____
_____
_____
_____

Daily Gratitude

Date:_____

_____
_____
_____
_____
_____

Date:_____

_____
_____
_____
_____
_____

Date:_____

_____
_____
_____
_____
_____

Date:_____

_____
_____
_____
_____
_____

Date:_____

_____
_____
_____
_____
_____

Date:_____

_____
_____
_____
_____
_____

Date:_____

_____
_____
_____
_____
_____

Date:_____

_____
_____
_____
_____
_____

Daily Gratitude

Date:_____
_____
_____
_____
_____
_____

Date:_____
_____
_____
_____
_____
_____

Date:_____
_____
_____
_____
_____
_____

Date:_____
_____
_____
_____
_____
_____

Date:_____
_____
_____
_____
_____
_____

Date:_____
_____
_____
_____
_____
_____

Date:_____
_____
_____
_____
_____
_____

Date:_____
_____
_____
_____
_____
_____

Daily Gratitude

Date:_____

_____
_____
_____
_____
_____

Date:_____

_____
_____
_____
_____
_____

Date:_____

_____
_____
_____
_____
_____

Date:_____

_____
_____
_____
_____
_____

Date:_____

_____
_____
_____
_____
_____

Date:_____

_____
_____
_____
_____
_____

Date:_____

_____
_____
_____
_____
_____

Date:_____

_____
_____
_____
_____
_____

Daily Gratitude

Date:_____

_____
_____
_____
_____
_____

Date:_____

_____
_____
_____
_____
_____

Date:_____

_____
_____
_____
_____
_____

Date:_____

_____
_____
_____
_____
_____

Date:_____

_____
_____
_____
_____
_____

Date:_____

_____
_____
_____
_____
_____

Date:_____

_____
_____
_____
_____
_____

Date:_____

_____
_____
_____
_____
_____

Daily Gratitude

Date:_____

_____
_____
_____
_____
_____

Date:_____

_____
_____
_____
_____
_____

Date:_____

_____
_____
_____
_____
_____

Date:_____

_____
_____
_____
_____
_____

Date:_____

_____
_____
_____
_____
_____

Date:_____

_____
_____
_____
_____
_____

Date:_____

_____
_____
_____
_____
_____

Date:_____

_____
_____
_____
_____
_____

grace for today

Inspiration

foundation

gratitude

grace

top 3 tasks

to do

Month of _____

Monthly Focus

Reminders

_____
_____
_____
_____
_____
_____
_____
_____
_____
_____
_____
_____
_____
_____
_____
_____
_____
_____
_____
_____
_____
_____
_____
_____
_____
_____
_____
_____
_____
_____
_____
_____
_____
_____
_____
_____
_____
_____
_____
_____
_____

top three things

1. _____
2. _____
3. _____
4.

Special Dates

_____
_____
_____
_____
_____

home keeping tasks

1. _____
2. _____
3. _____
4. _____

Goals

GOALS FOR THE MONTH

_____

_____ ☐
_____ ☐
_____ ☐
_____ ☐
_____ ☐
_____ ☐

_____

_____ ☐
_____ ☐
_____ ☐
_____ ☐
_____ ☐
_____ ☐

_____

_____ ☐
_____ ☐
_____ ☐
_____ ☐
_____ ☐
_____ ☐
_____ ☐

Daily Gratitude

Date:_____
_____
_____
_____
_____
_____

Date:_____
_____
_____
_____
_____
_____

Date:_____
_____
_____
_____
_____
_____

Date:_____
_____
_____
_____
_____
_____

Date:_____
_____
_____
_____
_____
_____

Date:_____
_____
_____
_____
_____
_____

Date:_____
_____
_____
_____
_____
_____

Date:_____
_____
_____
_____
_____
_____

Daily Gratitude

Date:_____

_____

_____

_____

_____

_____

Date:_____

_____

_____

_____

_____

_____

Date:_____

_____

_____

_____

_____

_____

Date:_____

_____

_____

_____

_____

_____

Date:_____

_____

_____

_____

_____

_____

Date:_____

_____

_____

_____

_____

_____

Date:_____

_____

_____

_____

_____

_____

Date:_____

_____

_____

_____

_____

_____

Daily Gratitude

Date:_____

_____

_____

_____

_____

_____

Date:_____

_____

_____

_____

_____

_____

Date:_____

_____

_____

_____

_____

_____

Date:_____

_____

_____

_____

_____

_____

Date:_____

_____

_____

_____

_____

_____

Date:_____

_____

_____

_____

_____

_____

Date:_____

_____

_____

_____

_____

_____

Date:_____

_____

_____

_____

_____

_____

Daily Gratitude

Date:_____

_____
_____
_____
_____

Date:_____

_____
_____
_____
_____

Date:_____

_____
_____
_____
_____

Date:_____

_____
_____
_____
_____

Date:_____

_____
_____
_____
_____

Date:_____

_____
_____
_____
_____

Date:_____

_____
_____
_____
_____
_____

Date:_____

_____
_____
_____
_____
_____

Daily Gratitude

Date:_____
_____
_____
_____
_____
_____

Date:_____
_____
_____
_____
_____
_____

Date:_____
_____
_____
_____
_____
_____

Date:_____
_____
_____
_____
_____
_____

Date:_____
_____
_____
_____
_____
_____

Date:_____
_____
_____
_____
_____
_____

Date:_____
_____
_____
_____
_____
_____

Date:_____
_____
_____
_____
_____
_____

Daily Gratitude

Date:_____

_____

_____

_____

_____

Date:_____

_____

_____

_____

_____

Date:_____

_____

_____

_____

_____

_____

Date:_____

_____

_____

_____

_____

_____

Date:_____

_____

_____

_____

_____

_____

Date:_____

_____

_____

_____

_____

_____

Date:_____

_____

_____

_____

_____

_____

Date:_____

_____

_____

_____

_____

_____

grace for today

Inspiration

foundation

gratitude

grace

top 3 tasks

to do

Month of _____

Monthly Focus

Reminders
_____
_____
_____
_____
_____
_____
_____
_____
_____
_____
_____
_____
_____
_____
_____
_____
_____
_____
_____
_____
_____
_____
_____
_____
_____
_____
_____
_____
_____
_____
_____
_____
_____
_____
_____
_____

top three things

1. _____

2. _____

3. _____

4.

Special Dates
_____
_____
_____
_____
_____
_____
_____
_____

home keeping tasks

1. _____

2. _____

3. _____

4. _____

Goals

GOALS FOR THE MONTH

_____ ☐
_____ ☐
_____ ☐
_____ ☐
_____ ☐
_____ ☐

_____ ☐
_____ ☐
_____ ☐
_____ ☐
_____ ☐
_____ ☐

_____ ☐
_____ ☐
_____ ☐
_____ ☐
_____ ☐
_____ ☐
_____ ☐

Daily Gratitude

Date:_____

_____
_____
_____
_____
_____

Date:_____

_____
_____
_____
_____
_____

Date:_____

_____
_____
_____
_____
_____

Date:_____

_____
_____
_____
_____
_____

Date:_____

_____
_____
_____
_____
_____

Date:_____

_____
_____
_____
_____
_____

Date:_____

_____
_____
_____
_____
_____

Date:_____

_____
_____
_____
_____
_____

Daily Gratitude

Date:_____

_____

_____

_____

_____

_____

Date:_____

_____

_____

_____

_____

_____

Date:_____

_____

_____

_____

_____

_____

Date:_____

_____

_____

_____

_____

_____

Date:_____

_____

_____

_____

_____

_____

Date:_____

_____

_____

_____

_____

_____

Date:_____

_____

_____

_____

_____

_____

Date:_____

_____

_____

_____

_____

_____

Daily Gratitude

Date:_____

_____
_____
_____
_____

Date:_____

_____
_____
_____
_____

Date:_____

_____
_____
_____
_____

Date:_____

_____
_____
_____
_____

Date:_____

_____
_____
_____
_____

Date:_____

_____
_____
_____
_____

Date:_____

_____
_____
_____
_____

Date:_____

_____
_____
_____
_____

Daily Gratitude

Date:_____

_____
_____
_____
_____
_____

Date:_____

_____
_____
_____
_____
_____

Date:_____

_____
_____
_____
_____
_____

Date:_____

_____
_____
_____
_____
_____

Date:_____

_____
_____
_____
_____
_____

Date:_____

_____
_____
_____
_____
_____

Date:_____

_____
_____
_____
_____
_____

Date:_____

_____
_____
_____
_____
_____

Daily Gratitude

Date:_____
_____
_____
_____
_____
_____

Date:_____
_____
_____
_____
_____
_____

Date:_____
_____
_____
_____
_____
_____

Date:_____
_____
_____
_____
_____
_____

Date:_____
_____
_____
_____
_____
_____

Date:_____
_____
_____
_____
_____
_____

Date:_____
_____
_____
_____
_____
_____

Date:_____
_____
_____
_____
_____
_____

Daily Gratitude

Date:_____

_____
_____
_____
_____
_____

Date:_____

_____
_____
_____
_____
_____

Date:_____

_____
_____
_____
_____
_____

Date:_____

_____
_____
_____
_____
_____

Date:_____

_____
_____
_____
_____
_____

Date:_____

_____
_____
_____
_____
_____

Date:_____

_____
_____
_____
_____
_____

Date:_____

_____
_____
_____
_____
_____

grace for today

Inspiration

foundation

gratitude

grace

top 3 tasks

to do

Month of _____

Monthly Focus

Reminders

_____
_____
_____
_____
_____
_____
_____
_____
_____
_____
_____
_____
_____
_____
_____
_____
_____
_____
_____
_____
_____
_____
_____
_____
_____
_____
_____
_____
_____
_____
_____
_____
_____
_____
_____

top three things

1. _____

2. _____

3. _____

4.

Special Dates

_____
_____
_____
_____
_____
_____
_____

home keeping tasks

1. _____

2. _____

3. _____

4. _____

Goals

GOALS FOR THE MONTH

- _____ ☐
- _____ ☐
- _____ ☐
- _____ ☐
- _____ ☐
- _____ ☐

- _____ ☐
- _____ ☐
- _____ ☐
- _____ ☐
- _____ ☐
- _____ ☐

- _____ ☐
- _____ ☐
- _____ ☐
- _____ ☐
- _____ ☐
- _____ ☐
- _____ ☐

Daily Gratitude

Date:_____

_____
_____
_____
_____
_____

Date:_____

_____
_____
_____
_____
_____

Date:_____

_____
_____
_____
_____
_____

Date:_____

_____
_____
_____
_____
_____

Date:_____

_____
_____
_____
_____
_____

Date:_____

_____
_____
_____
_____
_____

Date:_____

_____
_____
_____
_____
_____

Date:_____

_____
_____
_____
_____
_____

Daily Gratitude

Date:_____
_____
_____
_____
_____
_____

Date:_____
_____
_____
_____
_____
_____

Date:_____
_____
_____
_____
_____
_____

Date:_____
_____
_____
_____
_____
_____

Date:_____
_____
_____
_____
_____
_____

Date:_____
_____
_____
_____
_____
_____

Date:_____
_____
_____
_____
_____
_____

Date:_____
_____
_____
_____
_____
_____

Daily Gratitude

Date:_____

_____
_____
_____
_____

Date:_____

_____
_____
_____
_____

Date:_____

_____
_____
_____
_____

Date:_____

_____
_____
_____
_____

Date:_____

_____
_____
_____
_____

Date:_____

_____
_____
_____
_____

Date:_____

_____
_____
_____
_____

Date:_____

_____
_____
_____
_____

Daily Gratitude

Date:_____

_____
_____
_____
_____

Date:_____

_____
_____
_____
_____

Date:_____

_____
_____
_____
_____

Date:_____

_____
_____
_____
_____

Date:_____

_____
_____
_____
_____

Date:_____

_____
_____
_____
_____

Date:_____

_____
_____
_____
_____

Date:_____

_____
_____
_____
_____

Daily Gratitude

Date:_____

_____
_____
_____
_____
_____

Date:_____

_____
_____
_____
_____
_____

Date:_____

_____
_____
_____
_____
_____

Date:_____

_____
_____
_____
_____
_____

Date:_____

_____
_____
_____
_____
_____

Date:_____

_____
_____
_____
_____
_____

Date:_____

_____
_____
_____
_____
_____

Date:_____

_____
_____
_____
_____
_____

Daily Gratitude

Date:_____

_____

_____

_____

_____

_____

Date:_____

_____

_____

_____

_____

_____

Date:_____

_____

_____

_____

_____

_____

Date:_____

_____

_____

_____

_____

_____

Date:_____

_____

_____

_____

_____

_____

Date:_____

_____

_____

_____

_____

_____

Date:_____

_____

_____

_____

_____

_____

Date:_____

_____

_____

_____

_____

_____

grace for today

Inspiration

foundation

gratitude

grace

top 3 tasks

to do

Month of _____

Monthly Focus

Reminders

_____
_____
_____
_____
_____
_____
_____
_____
_____
_____
_____
_____
_____
_____
_____
_____
_____
_____
_____
_____
_____
_____
_____
_____
_____
_____
_____
_____
_____
_____
_____
_____
_____
_____
_____
_____
_____
_____
_____

top three things

1. _____

2. _____

3. _____

4.

Special Dates

_____
_____
_____
_____
_____
_____
_____
_____

home keeping tasks

1. _____

2. _____

3. _____

4. _____

Goals

GOALS FOR THE MONTH

- _____ ☐
- _____ ☐
- _____ ☐
- _____ ☐
- _____ ☐
- _____ ☐

- _____ ☐
- _____ ☐
- _____ ☐
- _____ ☐
- _____ ☐
- _____ ☐

- _____ ☐
- _____ ☐
- _____ ☐
- _____ ☐
- _____ ☐
- _____ ☐
- _____ ☐

Daily Gratitude

Date:_____

_____
_____
_____
_____
_____

Date:_____

_____
_____
_____
_____
_____

Date:_____

_____
_____
_____
_____
_____

Date:_____

_____
_____
_____
_____
_____

Date:_____

_____
_____
_____
_____
_____

Date:_____

_____
_____
_____
_____
_____

Date:_____

_____
_____
_____
_____
_____

Date:_____

_____
_____
_____
_____
_____

Daily Gratitude

Date:_____

_____
_____
_____
_____
_____

Date:_____

_____
_____
_____
_____
_____

Date:_____

_____
_____
_____
_____
_____

Date:_____

_____
_____
_____
_____
_____

Date:_____

_____
_____
_____
_____
_____

Date:_____

_____
_____
_____
_____
_____

Date:_____

_____
_____
_____
_____
_____

Date:_____

_____
_____
_____
_____
_____

Daily Gratitude

Date:_____
_____
_____
_____
_____

Date:_____
_____
_____
_____
_____

Date:_____
_____
_____
_____
_____

Date:_____
_____
_____
_____
_____

Date:_____
_____
_____
_____
_____

Date:_____
_____
_____
_____
_____

Date:_____
_____
_____
_____
_____

Date:_____
_____
_____
_____
_____

Daily Gratitude

Date:_____

_____
_____
_____
_____
_____

Date:_____

_____
_____
_____
_____
_____

Date:_____

_____
_____
_____
_____
_____

Date:_____

_____
_____
_____
_____
_____

Date:_____

_____
_____
_____
_____
_____

Date:_____

_____
_____
_____
_____
_____

Date:_____

_____
_____
_____
_____
_____

Date:_____

_____
_____
_____
_____
_____

Daily Gratitude

Date:_____

_____

_____

_____

_____

_____

Date:_____

_____

_____

_____

_____

_____

Date:_____

_____

_____

_____

_____

_____

Date:_____

_____

_____

_____

_____

_____

Date:_____

_____

_____

_____

_____

_____

Date:_____

_____

_____

_____

_____

_____

Date:_____

_____

_____

_____

_____

_____

Date:_____

_____

_____

_____

_____

_____

Daily Gratitude

Date:_____

_____
_____
_____
_____
_____

Date:_____

_____
_____
_____
_____
_____

Date:_____

_____
_____
_____
_____
_____

Date:_____

_____
_____
_____
_____
_____

Date:_____

_____
_____
_____
_____
_____

Date:_____

_____
_____
_____
_____
_____

Date:_____

_____
_____
_____
_____
_____

Date:_____

_____
_____
_____
_____
_____

grace for today

Inspiration

foundation

gratitude

grace

top 3 tasks

to do

Month of _____

Monthly Focus

Reminders

_____
_____
_____
_____
_____
_____
_____
_____
_____
_____
_____
_____
_____
_____
_____
_____
_____
_____
_____
_____
_____
_____
_____
_____
_____
_____
_____
_____
_____
_____
_____
_____
_____

top three things

1. _____
2. _____
3. _____
4.

Special Dates

_____
_____
_____
_____
_____
_____
_____
_____

home keeping tasks

1. _____
2. _____
3. _____
4. _____

Goals

GOALS FOR THE MONTH

_____ ☐

_____ ☐

_____ ☐

_____ ☐

_____ ☐

_____ ☐

_____ ☐

_____ ☐

_____ ☐

_____ ☐

_____ ☐

_____ ☐

_____ ☐

_____ ☐

_____ ☐

_____ ☐

_____ ☐

_____ ☐

_____ ☐

Daily Gratitude

Date:_____

_____
_____
_____
_____
_____

Date:_____

_____
_____
_____
_____
_____

Date:_____

_____
_____
_____
_____
_____

Date:_____

_____
_____
_____
_____
_____

Date:_____

_____
_____
_____
_____
_____

Date:_____

_____
_____
_____
_____
_____

Date:_____

_____
_____
_____
_____
_____

Date:_____

_____
_____
_____
_____
_____

Daily Gratitude

Date:_____

_____
_____
_____
_____
_____

Date:_____

_____
_____
_____
_____
_____

Date:_____

_____
_____
_____
_____
_____

Date:_____

_____
_____
_____
_____
_____

Date:_____

_____
_____
_____
_____
_____

Date:_____

_____
_____
_____
_____
_____

Date:_____

_____
_____
_____
_____
_____

Date:_____

_____
_____
_____
_____
_____

Daily Gratitude

Date:_____

_____
_____
_____
_____
_____

Date:_____

_____
_____
_____
_____
_____

Date:_____

_____
_____
_____
_____
_____

Date:_____

_____
_____
_____
_____
_____

Date:_____

_____
_____
_____
_____
_____

Date:_____

_____
_____
_____
_____
_____

Date:_____

_____
_____
_____
_____
_____

Date:_____

_____
_____
_____
_____
_____

Daily Gratitude

Date:_____
_____
_____
_____
_____
_____

Date:_____
_____
_____
_____
_____
_____

Date:_____
_____
_____
_____
_____
_____

Date:_____
_____
_____
_____
_____
_____

Date:_____
_____
_____
_____
_____
_____

Date:_____
_____
_____
_____
_____
_____

Date:_____
_____
_____
_____
_____
_____

Date:_____
_____
_____
_____
_____
_____

Daily Gratitude

Date:_____
_____
_____
_____
_____
_____

Date:_____
_____
_____
_____
_____
_____

Date:_____
_____
_____
_____
_____
_____

Date:_____
_____
_____
_____
_____
_____

Date:_____
_____
_____
_____
_____
_____

Date:_____
_____
_____
_____
_____
_____

Date:_____
_____
_____
_____
_____
_____

Date:_____
_____
_____
_____
_____
_____

Daily Gratitude

Date:_____
_____
_____
_____
_____
_____

Date:_____
_____
_____
_____
_____
_____

Date:_____
_____
_____
_____
_____
_____

Date:_____
_____
_____
_____
_____
_____

Date:_____
_____
_____
_____
_____
_____

Date:_____
_____
_____
_____
_____
_____

Date:_____
_____
_____
_____
_____
_____

Date:_____
_____
_____
_____
_____
_____

grace for today

Inspiration

top 3 tasks

foundation

gratitude

to do

grace

Month of _____

Monthly Focus

Reminders

_____
_____
_____
_____
_____
_____
_____
_____
_____
_____
_____
_____
_____
_____
_____
_____
_____
_____
_____
_____
_____
_____
_____
_____
_____
_____
_____
_____
_____
_____
_____
_____

top three things

1. _____

2. _____

3. _____

4.

Special Dates

_____
_____
_____
_____
_____
_____
_____

home keeping tasks

1. _____

2. _____

3. _____

4. _____

Goals

GOALS FOR THE MONTH

_____

_____ ☐

_____ ☐

_____ ☐

_____ ☐

_____ ☐

_____ ☐

_____

_____ ☐

_____ ☐

_____ ☐

_____ ☐

_____ ☐

_____ ☐

_____

_____ ☐

_____ ☐

_____ ☐

_____ ☐

_____ ☐

_____ ☐

_____ ☐

Daily Gratitude

Date:_____
_____
_____
_____
_____
_____

Date:_____
_____
_____
_____
_____
_____

Date:_____
_____
_____
_____
_____
_____

Date:_____
_____
_____
_____
_____
_____

Date:_____
_____
_____
_____
_____
_____

Date:_____
_____
_____
_____
_____
_____

Date:_____
_____
_____
_____
_____
_____

Date:_____
_____
_____
_____
_____
_____

Daily Gratitude

Date:_____
_____
_____
_____
_____
_____

Date:_____
_____
_____
_____
_____
_____

Date:_____
_____
_____
_____
_____
_____

Date:_____
_____
_____
_____
_____
_____

Date:_____
_____
_____
_____
_____
_____

Date:_____
_____
_____
_____
_____
_____

Date:_____
_____
_____
_____
_____
_____

Date:_____
_____
_____
_____
_____
_____

Daily Gratitude

Date:_____

_____
_____
_____
_____
_____

Date:_____

_____
_____
_____
_____
_____

Date:_____

_____
_____
_____
_____
_____

Date:_____

_____
_____
_____
_____
_____

Date:_____

_____
_____
_____
_____
_____

Date:_____

_____
_____
_____
_____
_____

Date:_____

_____
_____
_____
_____
_____

Date:_____

_____
_____
_____
_____
_____

Daily Gratitude

Date:_____

_____
_____
_____
_____
_____

Date:_____

_____
_____
_____
_____
_____

Date:_____

_____
_____
_____
_____
_____

Date:_____

_____
_____
_____
_____
_____

Date:_____

_____
_____
_____
_____
_____

Date:_____

_____
_____
_____
_____
_____

Date:_____

_____
_____
_____
_____
_____

Date:_____

_____
_____
_____
_____
_____

Daily Gratitude

Date:_____

_____

_____

_____

_____

_____

Date:_____

_____

_____

_____

_____

_____

Date:_____

_____

_____

_____

_____

_____

Date:_____

_____

_____

_____

_____

_____

Date:_____

_____

_____

_____

_____

_____

Date:_____

_____

_____

_____

_____

_____

Date:_____

_____

_____

_____

_____

_____

Date:_____

_____

_____

_____

_____

_____

Daily Gratitude

Date:_____

_____
_____
_____
_____

Date:_____

_____
_____
_____
_____

Date:_____

_____
_____
_____
_____

Date:_____

_____
_____
_____
_____

Date:_____

_____
_____
_____
_____

Date:_____

_____
_____
_____
_____

Date:_____

_____
_____
_____
_____

Date:_____

_____
_____
_____
_____

grace for today

Inspiration

top 3 tasks

foundation

gratitude

to do

grace

Month of _____

Monthly Focus

Reminders

_____
_____
_____
_____
_____
_____
_____
_____
_____
_____
_____
_____
_____
_____
_____
_____
_____
_____
_____
_____
_____
_____
_____
_____
_____
_____
_____
_____
_____
_____
_____

top three things

1. _____

2. _____

3. _____

4.

Special Dates

_____
_____
_____
_____
_____
_____
_____
_____

home keeping tasks

1. _____

2. _____

3. _____

4. _____

Goals

GOALS FOR THE MONTH

_____

_____ ☐
_____ ☐
_____ ☐
_____ ☐
_____ ☐
_____ ☐

_____

_____ ☐
_____ ☐
_____ ☐
_____ ☐
_____ ☐
_____ ☐

_____

_____ ☐
_____ ☐
_____ ☐
_____ ☐
_____ ☐
_____ ☐
_____ ☐

Daily Gratitude

Date:_____

_____
_____
_____
_____
_____

Date:_____

_____
_____
_____
_____
_____

Date:_____

_____
_____
_____
_____
_____

Date:_____

_____
_____
_____
_____
_____

Date:_____

_____
_____
_____
_____
_____

Date:_____

_____
_____
_____
_____
_____

Date:_____

_____
_____
_____
_____
_____

Date:_____

_____
_____
_____
_____
_____

Daily Gratitude

Date:_____
_____
_____
_____
_____
_____

Date:_____
_____
_____
_____
_____
_____

Date:_____
_____
_____
_____
_____
_____

Date:_____
_____
_____
_____
_____
_____

Date:_____
_____
_____
_____
_____
_____

Date:_____
_____
_____
_____
_____
_____

Date:_____
_____
_____
_____
_____
_____

Date:_____
_____
_____
_____
_____
_____

Daily Gratitude

Date:_____

_____
_____
_____
_____

Date:_____

_____
_____
_____
_____

Date:_____

_____
_____
_____
_____

Date:_____

_____
_____
_____
_____

Date:_____

_____
_____
_____
_____

Date:_____

_____
_____
_____
_____

Date:_____

_____
_____
_____
_____

Date:_____

_____
_____
_____
_____

Daily Gratitude

Date:_____

_____
_____
_____
_____
_____

Date:_____

_____
_____
_____
_____
_____

Date:_____

_____
_____
_____
_____
_____

Date:_____

_____
_____
_____
_____
_____

Date:_____

_____
_____
_____
_____
_____

Date:_____

_____
_____
_____
_____
_____

Date:_____

_____
_____
_____
_____
_____

Date:_____

_____
_____
_____
_____
_____

Daily Gratitude

Date:_____

_____
_____
_____
_____
_____

Date:_____

_____
_____
_____
_____
_____

Date:_____

_____
_____
_____
_____
_____

Date:_____

_____
_____
_____
_____
_____

Date:_____

_____
_____
_____
_____
_____

Date:_____

_____
_____
_____
_____
_____

Date:_____

_____
_____
_____
_____
_____

Date:_____

_____
_____
_____
_____
_____

Daily Gratitude

Date:_____

_____

_____

_____

_____

_____

Date:_____

_____

_____

_____

_____

_____

Date:_____

_____

_____

_____

_____

_____

Date:_____

_____

_____

_____

_____

_____

Date:_____

_____

_____

_____

_____

_____

Date:_____

_____

_____

_____

_____

_____

Date:_____

_____

_____

_____

_____

_____

Date:_____

_____

_____

_____

_____

_____

grace for today

Inspiration

top 3 tasks

foundation

gratitude

to do

grace

Month of _____

Monthly Focus

Reminders

_____
_____
_____
_____
_____
_____
_____
_____
_____
_____
_____
_____
_____
_____
_____
_____
_____
_____
_____
_____
_____
_____
_____
_____
_____
_____
_____
_____
_____

top three things

1. _____
2. _____
3. _____
4.

Special Dates

_____
_____
_____
_____
_____
_____
_____

home keeping tasks

1. _____
2. _____
3. _____
4. _____

Goals

GOALS FOR THE MONTH

_____ ☐

_____ ☐

_____ ☐

_____ ☐

_____ ☐

_____ ☐

_____ ☐

_____ ☐

_____ ☐

_____ ☐

_____ ☐

_____ ☐

_____ ☐

_____ ☐

_____ ☐

_____ ☐

_____ ☐

_____ ☐

_____ ☐

Daily Gratitude

Date:_____

_____

_____

_____

_____

Date:_____

_____

_____

_____

_____

Date:_____

_____

_____

_____

_____

_____

Date:_____

_____

_____

_____

_____

_____

Date:_____

_____

_____

_____

_____

_____

Date:_____

_____

_____

_____

_____

_____

Date:_____

_____

_____

_____

_____

_____

Date:_____

_____

_____

_____

_____

_____

Daily Gratitude

Date:_____
_____
_____
_____
_____
_____

Date:_____
_____
_____
_____
_____
_____

Date:_____
_____
_____
_____
_____
_____

Date:_____
_____
_____
_____
_____
_____

Date:_____
_____
_____
_____
_____
_____

Date:_____
_____
_____
_____
_____
_____

Date:_____
_____
_____
_____
_____
_____

Date:_____
_____
_____
_____
_____
_____

Daily Gratitude

Date:_____
_____
_____
_____
_____

Date:_____
_____
_____
_____
_____

Date:_____
_____
_____
_____
_____

Date:_____
_____
_____
_____
_____

Date:_____
_____
_____
_____
_____

Date:_____
_____
_____
_____
_____

Date:_____
_____
_____
_____
_____

Date:_____
_____
_____
_____
_____

Daily Gratitude

Date:_____

_____
_____
_____
_____
_____

Date:_____

_____
_____
_____
_____
_____

Date:_____

_____
_____
_____
_____
_____

Date:_____

_____
_____
_____
_____
_____

Date:_____

_____
_____
_____
_____
_____

Date:_____

_____
_____
_____
_____
_____

Date:_____

_____
_____
_____
_____
_____

Date:_____

_____
_____
_____
_____
_____

Daily Gratitude

Date:_____

_____
_____
_____
_____
_____

Date:_____

_____
_____
_____
_____
_____

Date:_____

_____
_____
_____
_____
_____

Date:_____

_____
_____
_____
_____
_____

Date:_____

_____
_____
_____
_____
_____

Date:_____

_____
_____
_____
_____
_____

Date:_____

_____
_____
_____
_____
_____

Date:_____

_____
_____
_____
_____
_____

Daily Gratitude

Date:_____

_____
_____
_____
_____
_____

Date:_____

_____
_____
_____
_____
_____

Date:_____

_____
_____
_____
_____
_____

Date:_____

_____
_____
_____
_____
_____

Date:_____

_____
_____
_____
_____
_____

Date:_____

_____
_____
_____
_____
_____

Date:_____

_____
_____
_____
_____
_____

Date:_____

_____
_____
_____
_____
_____

grace for today

Inspiration

top 3 tasks

foundation

gratitude

to do

grace

Month of _____

Monthly Focus

Reminders

_____
_____
_____
_____
_____
_____
_____
_____
_____
_____
_____
_____
_____
_____
_____
_____
_____
_____
_____
_____
_____
_____
_____
_____
_____
_____
_____
_____
_____
_____
_____
_____
_____
_____
_____
_____
_____
_____
_____

top three things

1. _____

2. _____

3. _____

4.

Special Dates

_____
_____
_____
_____
_____
_____
_____

home keeping tasks

1. _____

2. _____

3. _____

4. _____

Goals

GOALS FOR THE MONTH

_____ ☐
_____ ☐
_____ ☐
_____ ☐
_____ ☐
_____ ☐

_____ ☐
_____ ☐
_____ ☐
_____ ☐
_____ ☐
_____ ☐

_____ ☐
_____ ☐
_____ ☐
_____ ☐
_____ ☐
_____ ☐
_____ ☐

Daily Gratitude

Date:_____

_____
_____
_____
_____
_____

Date:_____

_____
_____
_____
_____
_____

Date:_____

_____
_____
_____
_____
_____

Date:_____

_____
_____
_____
_____
_____

Date:_____

_____
_____
_____
_____
_____

Date:_____

_____
_____
_____
_____
_____

Date:_____

_____
_____
_____
_____
_____

Date:_____

_____
_____
_____
_____
_____

Daily Gratitude

Date:_____

_____
_____
_____
_____
_____

Date:_____

_____
_____
_____
_____
_____

Date:_____

_____
_____
_____
_____
_____

Date:_____

_____
_____
_____
_____
_____

Date:_____

_____
_____
_____
_____
_____

Date:_____

_____
_____
_____
_____
_____

Date:_____

_____
_____
_____
_____
_____

Date:_____

_____
_____
_____
_____
_____

Daily Gratitude

Date:_____

_____
_____
_____
_____
_____

Date:_____

_____
_____
_____
_____
_____

Date:_____

_____
_____
_____
_____
_____

Date:_____

_____
_____
_____
_____
_____

Date:_____

_____
_____
_____
_____
_____

Date:_____

_____
_____
_____
_____
_____

Date:_____

_____
_____
_____
_____
_____

Date:_____

_____
_____
_____
_____
_____

Daily Gratitude

Date:_____

_____
_____
_____
_____
_____

Date:_____

_____
_____
_____
_____
_____

Date:_____

_____
_____
_____
_____
_____

Date:_____

_____
_____
_____
_____
_____

Date:_____

_____
_____
_____
_____
_____

Date:_____

_____
_____
_____
_____
_____

Date:_____

_____
_____
_____
_____
_____

Date:_____

_____
_____
_____
_____
_____

Daily Gratitude

Date:_____

_____
_____
_____
_____
_____

Date:_____

_____
_____
_____
_____
_____

Date:_____

_____
_____
_____
_____
_____

Date:_____

_____
_____
_____
_____
_____

Date:_____

_____
_____
_____
_____
_____

Date:_____

_____
_____
_____
_____
_____

Date:_____

_____
_____
_____
_____
_____

Date:_____

_____
_____
_____
_____
_____

Daily Gratitude

Date:_____

_____
_____
_____
_____
_____

Date:_____

_____
_____
_____
_____
_____

Date:_____

_____
_____
_____
_____
_____

Date:_____

_____
_____
_____
_____
_____

Date:_____

_____
_____
_____
_____
_____

Date:_____

_____
_____
_____
_____
_____

Date:_____

_____
_____
_____
_____
_____

Date:_____

_____
_____
_____
_____
_____

grace for today

Inspiration

foundation

gratitude

grace

top 3 tasks

to do

Month of _____

Monthly Focus

Reminders

_____
_____
_____
_____
_____
_____
_____
_____
_____
_____
_____
_____
_____
_____
_____
_____
_____
_____
_____
_____
_____
_____
_____
_____
_____
_____
_____
_____
_____
_____
_____
_____
_____
_____
_____

top three things

1. _____

2. _____

3. _____

4.

Special Dates

_____
_____
_____
_____
_____
_____
_____

home keeping tasks

1. _____

2. _____

3. _____

4. _____

Goals

GOALS FOR THE MONTH

_____

_____ ☐
_____ ☐
_____ ☐
_____ ☐
_____ ☐
_____ ☐

_____

_____ ☐
_____ ☐
_____ ☐
_____ ☐
_____ ☐
_____ ☐

_____

_____ ☐
_____ ☐
_____ ☐
_____ ☐
_____ ☐
_____ ☐
_____ ☐

Daily Gratitude

Date:_____
_____
_____
_____
_____
_____

Date:_____
_____
_____
_____
_____
_____

Date:_____
_____
_____
_____
_____
_____

Date:_____
_____
_____
_____
_____
_____

Date:_____
_____
_____
_____
_____
_____

Date:_____
_____
_____
_____
_____
_____

Date:_____
_____
_____
_____
_____
_____

Date:_____
_____
_____
_____
_____
_____

Daily Gratitude

Date:_____

_____
_____
_____
_____
_____

Date:_____

_____
_____
_____
_____
_____

Date:_____

_____
_____
_____
_____
_____

Date:_____

_____
_____
_____
_____
_____

Date:_____

_____
_____
_____
_____
_____

Date:_____

_____
_____
_____
_____
_____

Date:_____

_____
_____
_____
_____
_____

Date:_____

_____
_____
_____
_____
_____

Daily Gratitude

Date:_____
_____
_____
_____
_____
_____

Date:_____
_____
_____
_____
_____
_____

Date:_____
_____
_____
_____
_____
_____

Date:_____
_____
_____
_____
_____
_____

Date:_____
_____
_____
_____
_____
_____

Date:_____
_____
_____
_____
_____
_____

Date:_____
_____
_____
_____
_____
_____

Date:_____
_____
_____
_____
_____
_____

Daily Gratitude

Date:_____

_____

_____

_____

_____

_____

Date:_____

_____

_____

_____

_____

_____

Date:_____

_____

_____

_____

_____

_____

Date:_____

_____

_____

_____

_____

_____

Date:_____

_____

_____

_____

_____

_____

Date:_____

_____

_____

_____

_____

_____

Date:_____

_____

_____

_____

_____

_____

Date:_____

_____

_____

_____

_____

_____

Daily Gratitude

Date:_____

_____
_____
_____
_____
_____

Date:_____

_____
_____
_____
_____
_____

Date:_____

_____
_____
_____
_____
_____

Date:_____

_____
_____
_____
_____
_____

Date:_____

_____
_____
_____
_____
_____

Date:_____

_____
_____
_____
_____
_____

Date:_____

_____
_____
_____
_____
_____

Date:_____

_____
_____
_____
_____
_____

Daily Gratitude

Date:_____

_____
_____
_____
_____
_____

Date:_____

_____
_____
_____
_____
_____

Date:_____

_____
_____
_____
_____
_____

Date:_____

_____
_____
_____
_____
_____

Date:_____

_____
_____
_____
_____
_____

Date:_____

_____
_____
_____
_____
_____

Date:_____

_____
_____
_____
_____
_____

Date:_____

_____
_____
_____
_____
_____

grace for today

Inspiration

top 3 tasks

foundation

gratitude

to do

grace

www.ingramcontent.com/pod-product-compliance
Lightning Source LLC
Chambersburg PA
CBHW081333090426
42737CB00017B/3130